FOREWORD

The collection of "Everything Will Be Okay" travel phrasebooks published by T&P Books is designed for people traveling abroad for tourism and business. The phrasebooks contain what matters most - the essentials for basic communication. This is an indispensable set of phrases to "survive" while abroad.

This phrasebook will help you in most cases where you need to ask something, get directions, find out how much something costs, etc. It can also resolve difficult communication situations where gestures just won't help.

This book contains a lot of phrases that have been grouped according to the most relevant topics. You'll also find a mini dictionary with useful words - numbers, time, calendar, colors…

Take "Everything Will Be Okay" phrasebook with you on the road and you'll have an irreplaceable traveling companion who will help you find your way out of any situation and teach you to not fear speaking with foreigners.

TABLE OF CONTENTS

T&P Books Publishing

PHRASEBOOK

— KOREAN —

By Andrey Taranov

THE MOST IMPORTANT PHRASES

This phrasebook contains
the most important
phrases and questions
for basic communication
Everything you need
to survive overseas

T&P BOOKS

Phrasebook + 250-word dictionary

English-Korean phrasebook & mini dictionary

By Andrey Taranov

The collection of "Everything Will Be Okay" travel phrasebooks published by T&P Books is designed for people traveling abroad for tourism and business. The phrasebooks contain what matters most - the essentials for basic communication. This is an indispensable set of phrases to "survive" while abroad.

You'll also find a mini dictionary with 250 useful words required for everyday communication - the names of months and days of the week, measurements, family members, and more.

T&P Books Publishing
www.tpbooks.com

ISBN: 978-1-78616-746-0

This book is also available in E-book formats.
Please visit www.tpbooks.com or the major online bookstores.

PRONUNCIATION

Letter	Korean example	T&P phonetic alphabet	English example

Consonants

Letter	Korean example	T&P phonetic alphabet	English example
ㄱ [1]	개	[k]	clock, kiss
ㄱ [2]	아기	[g]	game, gold
ㄲ	껌	[k]	tense [k]
ㄴ	눈	[n]	name, normal
ㄷ [3]	달	[t]	tourist, trip
ㄷ [4]	사다리	[d]	day, doctor
ㄸ	딸	[t]	tense [t]
ㄹ [5]	라디오	[r]	rice, radio
ㄹ [6]	십팔	[l]	lace, people
ㅁ	문	[m]	magic, milk
ㅂ [7]	봄	[p]	pencil, private
ㅂ [8]	아버지	[b]	baby, book
ㅃ	빵	[p]	tense [p]
ㅅ [9]	실	[s]	city, boss
ㅅ [10]	옷	[t]	tourist, trip
ㅆ	쌀	[ja:]	royal
ㅇ [11]	강	[ng]	language, single
ㅈ [12]	집	[tɕ]	cheer
ㅈ [13]	아주	[dʑ]	jeans, gene
ㅉ	짬	[tɕ]	tense [tch]
ㅊ	차	[tɕh]	hitchhiker
ㅌ	택시	[th]	don't have
ㅋ	칼	[kh]	work hard
ㅍ	포도	[ph]	top hat
ㅎ	한국	[h]	home, have

Letter	Korean example	T&P phonetic alphabet	English example

Vowels and combinations with vowels

Letter	Korean example	T&P phonetic alphabet	English example
ㅏ	사	[a]	shorter than in ask
ㅑ	향	[ja]	Kenya, piano
ㅓ	머리	[ʌ]	lucky, sun
ㅕ	병	[jɑ]	young, yard
ㅗ	몸	[o]	pod, John
ㅛ	표	[jɔ]	New York
ㅜ	물	[u]	book
ㅠ	슈퍼	[ju]	youth, usually
ㅡ	음악	[ɪ]	big, America
ㅣ	길	[i], [iː]	feet, Peter
ㅐ	뱀	[ɛ], [ɛː]	habit, bad
ㅒ	애기	[je]	yesterday, yen
ㅔ	펜	[e]	elm, medal
ㅖ	계산	[je]	yesterday, yen
ㅘ	왕	[wa]	watt, white
ㅙ	왜	[ʊə]	pure, fuel
ㅚ	회의	[ø], [we]	first, web
ㅝ	권	[uɔ]	to order, to open
ㅞ	웬	[ʊə]	pure, fuel
ㅟ	쥐	[wi]	whiskey
ㅢ	거의	[ɰi]	combination [ɪi]

Comments

[1] at the beginning of words
[2] between voiced sounds
[3] at the beginning of words
[4] between voiced sounds
[5] at the beginning of a syllable
[6] at the end of a syllable
[7] at the beginning of words
[8] between voiced sounds
[9] at the beginning of a syllable
[10] at the end of a syllable
[11] at the end of a syllable
[12] at the beginning of words
[13] between voiced sounds

LIST OF ABBREVIATIONS

English abbreviations

ab.	-	about
adj	-	adjective
adv	-	adverb
anim.	-	animate
as adj	-	attributive noun used as adjective
e.g.	-	for example
etc.	-	et cetera
fam.	-	familiar
fem.	-	feminine
form.	-	formal
inanim.	-	inanimate
masc.	-	masculine
math	-	mathematics
mil.	-	military
n	-	noun
pl	-	plural
pron.	-	pronoun
sb	-	somebody
sing.	-	singular
sth	-	something
v aux	-	auxiliary verb
vi	-	intransitive verb
vi, vt	-	intransitive, transitive verb
vt	-	transitive verb

T&P BOOKS

KOREAN PHRASEBOOK

This section contains important phrases that may come in handy in various real-life situations.
The phrasebook will help you ask for directions, clarify a price, buy tickets, and order food at a restaurant

T&P Books Publishing

PHRASEBOOK
CONTENTS

T&P Books Publishing

The bare minimum

Excuse me, ...	실례합니다, ··· sil-lye-ham-ni-da, ...
Hello.	안녕하세요. an-nyeong-ha-se-yo.
Thank you.	감사합니다. gam-sa-ham-ni-da.
Good bye.	안녕히 계세요. an-nyeong-hi gye-se-yo.
Yes.	네. ne.
No.	아니오. a-ni-o.
I don't know.	모르겠어요. mo-reu-ge-seo-yo.
Where? | Where to? | When?	어디예요? | 어디까지 가세요? | 언제요? eo-di-ye-yo? | eo-di-kka-ji ga-se-yo? | eon-je-yo?

I need ...	··· 필요해요. ... pi-ryo-hae-yo.
I want ...	··· 싶어요. ... si-peo-yo.
Do you have ...?	··· 있으세요? ... i-seu-se-yo?
Is there a ... here?	여기 ··· 있어요? yeo-gi ... i-seo-yo?
May I ...?	···해도 되나요? ... hae-do doe-na-yo?
..., please (polite request)	···, 부탁합니다. ..., bu-tak-am-ni-da.

I'm looking for ...	··· 찾고 있어요. ... chat-go i-seo-yo.
restroom	화장실 hwa-jang-sil
ATM	현금인출기 hyeon-geum-in-chul-gi
pharmacy (drugstore)	약국 yak-guk
hospital	병원 byeong-won
police station	경찰서 gyeong-chal-seo

subway	지하철 ji-ha-cheol
taxi	택시 taek-si
train station	기차역 gi-cha-yeok

My name is ...	제 이름은 … 입니다. je i-reu-meun ... im-ni-da.
What's your name?	성함이 어떻게 되세요? seong-ham-i eo-tteo-ke doe-se-yo?
Could you please help me?	도와주세요. do-wa-ju-se-yo.
I've got a problem.	문제가 있어요. mun-je-ga i-seo-yo.
I don't feel well.	몸이 안 좋아요. mom-i an jo-a-yo.
Call an ambulance!	구급차를 불러 주세요! gu-geup-cha-reul bul-leo ju-se-yo!
May I make a call?	전화를 써도 되나요? jeon-hwa-reul sseo-do doe-na-yo?

I'm sorry.	죄송합니다. joe-song-ham-ni-da.
You're welcome.	천만에요. cheon-man-e-yo.

I, me	저 jeo
you (inform.)	너 neo
he	그 geu
she	그녀 geu-nyeo
they (masc.)	그들 geu-deul
they (fem.)	그들 geu-deul
we	우리 u-ri
you (pl)	너희 neo-hui
you (sg, form.)	당신 dang-sin

ENTRANCE	입구 ip-gu
EXIT	출구 chul-gu
OUT OF ORDER	고장 go-jang

CLOSED	닫힘
	da-chim
OPEN	열림
	yeol-lim
FOR WOMEN	여성용
	yeo-seong-yong
FOR MEN	남성용
	nam-seong-yong

Questions

Where?
어디예요?
eo-di-ye-yo?

Where to?
어디까지 가세요?
eo-di-kka-ji ga-se-yo?

Where from?
어디에서요?
eo-di-e-seo-yo?

Why?
왜요?
wae-yo?

For what reason?
무슨 이유에서요?
mu-seun i-yu-e-seo-yo?

When?
언제요?
eon-je-yo?

How long?
얼마나요?
eol-ma-na-yo?

At what time?
몇 시에요?
myeot si-e-yo?

How much?
얼마예요?
eol-ma-ye-yo?

Do you have ...?
… 있으세요?
... i-seu-se-yo?

Where is ...?
… 어디 있어요?
... eo-di i-seo-yo?

What time is it?
지금 몇 시예요?
ji-geum myeot si-ye-yo?

May I make a call?
전화를 써도 되나요?
jeon-hwa-reul sseo-do doe-na-yo?

Who's there?
누구세요?
nu-gu-se-yo?

Can I smoke here?
담배를 피워도 되나요?
dam-bae-reul pi-wo-do doe-na-yo?

May I ...?
… 되나요?
... doe-na-yo?

Needs

I'd like …	… 하고 싶어요. … ha-go si-peo-yo.
I don't want …	… 하기 싫어요. … ha-gi si-reo-yo.
I'm thirsty.	목이 말라요. mo-gi mal-la-yo.
I want to sleep.	자고 싶어요. ja-go si-peo-yo.
I want …	… 싶어요. … si-peo-yo.
to wash up	씻고 ssit-go
to brush my teeth	이를 닦고 i-reul dak-go
to rest a while	쉬고 swi-go
to change my clothes	옷을 갈아입고 os-eul ga-ra-ip-go
to go back to the hotel	호텔로 돌아가고 ho-tel-lo do-ra-ga-go
to buy …	… 사고 … sa-go
to go to …	…에 가고 …e ga-go
to visit …	…에 방문하고 …e bang-mun-ha-go
to meet with …	… 만나고 … man-na-go
to make a call	전화를 걸고 jeon-hwa-reul geol-go
I'm tired.	저는 지쳤어요. jeo-neun ji-chyeo-seo-yo.
We are tired.	우리는 지쳤어요. u-ri-neun ji-chyeo-seo-yo.
I'm cold.	추워요. chu-wo-yo.
I'm hot.	더워요. deo-wo-yo.
I'm OK.	괜찮아요. gwaen-cha-na-yo.

I need to make a call.

전화를 걸어야 해요.
jeon-hwa-reul geo-reo-ya hae-yo.

I need to go to the restroom.

화장실에 가야 해요.
hwa-jang-si-re ga-ya hae-yo.

I have to go.

가야 해요.
ga-ya hae-yo.

I have to go now.

지금 가야 해요.
ji-geum ga-ya hae-yo.

Asking for directions

Excuse me, ...	실례합니다, ··· sil-lye-ham-ni-da, ...
Where is ...?	··· 어디 있어요? ... eo-di i-seo-yo?
Which way is ...?	··· 어느 쪽이예요? ... eo-neu jjo-gi-ye-yo?
Could you help me, please?	도와주실 수 있어요? do-wa-ju-sil su i-seo-yo?

I'm looking for ...	··· 찾고 있어요. ... chat-go i-seo-yo.
I'm looking for the exit.	출구를 찾고 있어요. chul-gu-reul chat-go i-seo-yo.
I'm going to ...	···에 가고 있어요. ... e ga-go i-seo-yo.
Am I going the right way to ...?	···에 가는데 이 길이 맞아요? ...e ga-neun-de i gi-ri ma-ja-yo?

Is it far?	먼가요? meon-ga-yo?
Can I get there on foot?	걸어갈 수 있어요? geo-reo-gal su i-seo-yo?
Can you show me on the map?	지도에서 보여주실 수 있어요? ji-do-e-seo bo-yeo-ju-sil su i-seo-yo?
Show me where we are right now.	지금 우리가 있는 곳을 보여주세요. ji-geum u-ri-ga in-neun gos-eul bo-yeo-ju-se-yo.

Here	여기 yeo-gi
There	거기 geo-gi
This way	이 길 i gil

Turn right.	오른쪽으로 가세요. o-reun-jjo-geu-ro ga-se-yo.
Turn left.	왼쪽으로 가세요. oen-jjo-geu-ro ga-se-yo.
first (second, third) turn	첫 번째 (두 번째, 세 번째) 골목 cheot beon-jjae (du beon-jjae, se beon-jjae) gol-mok

to the right

오른쪽으로
o-reun-jjo-geu-ro

to the left

왼쪽으로
oen-jjo-geu-ro

Go straight ahead.

직진하세요.
jik-jin-ha-se-yo.

Signs

WELCOME!	환영! hwa-nyeong!
ENTRANCE	입구 ip-gu
EXIT	출구 chul-gu
PUSH	미세요 mi-se-yo
PULL	당기세요 dang-gi-se-yo
OPEN	열림 yeol-lim
CLOSED	닫힘 da-chim
FOR WOMEN	여성용 yeo-seong-yong
FOR MEN	남성용 nam-seong-yong
GENTLEMEN, GENTS (m)	남성 (남) nam-seong (nam)
WOMEN (f)	여성 (여) yeo-seong (yeo)
DISCOUNTS	할인 ha-rin
SALE	세일 se-il
FREE	무료 mu-ryo
NEW!	신상품! sin-sang-pum!
ATTENTION!	주의! ju-ui!
NO VACANCIES	빈 방 없음 bin bang eop-seum
RESERVED	예약석 ye-yak-seok
ADMINISTRATION	사무실 sa-mu-sil
STAFF ONLY	직원 전용 ji-gwon jeo-nyong

BEWARE OF THE DOG!	개조심! gae-jo-sim!
NO SMOKING!	금연! geu-myeon!
DO NOT TOUCH!	만지지 마세요! man-ji-ji ma-se-yo!
DANGEROUS	위험 wi-heom
DANGER	위험 wi-heom
HIGH VOLTAGE	고압 전류 go-ap jeol-lyu
NO SWIMMING!	수영금지! su-yeong-geum-ji!

OUT OF ORDER	고장 go-jang
FLAMMABLE	가연성 ga-yeon-seong
FORBIDDEN	금지 geum-ji
NO TRESPASSING!	무단횡단 금지 mu-dan-hoeng-dan geum-ji
WET PAINT	젖은 페인트 jeo-jeun pe-in-teu

CLOSED FOR RENOVATIONS	공사중 gong-sa-jung
WORKS AHEAD	전방 공사중 jeon-bang gong-sa-jung
DETOUR	우회 도로 u-hoe do-ro

Transportation. General phrases

plane	비행기 bi-haeng-gi
train	기차 gi-cha
bus	버스 beo-seu
ferry	페리 pe-ri
taxi	택시 taek-si
car	자동차 ja-dong-cha
schedule	시간표 si-gan-pyo
Where can I see the schedule?	시간표는 어디서 볼 수 있어요? si-gan-pyo-neun eo-di-seo bol su i-seo-yo?
workdays (weekdays)	평일 pyeong-il
weekends	주말 ju-mal
holidays	휴일 hyu-il
DEPARTURE	출발 chul-bal
ARRIVAL	도착 do-chak
DELAYED	지연 ji-yeon
CANCELLED	취소 chwi-so
next (train, etc.)	다음 da-eum
first	첫 번째 cheot beon-jjae
last	마지막 ma-ji-mak

When is the next ...?

다음 … 언제인가요?
da-eum ... eon-je-in-ga-yo?

When is the first ...?

첫 … 언제인가요?
cheot ... eon-je-in-ga-yo?

When is the last ...?

마지막 … 언제인가요?
ma-ji-mak ... eon-je-in-ga-yo?

transfer (change of trains, etc.)

환승
hwan-seung

to make a transfer

환승하다
hwan-seung-ha-da

Do I need to make a transfer?

환승해야 해요?
hwan-seung-hae-ya hae-yo?

Buying tickets

Where can I buy tickets?	표는 어디서 사나요? pyo-neun eo-di-seo sa-na-yo?
ticket	표 pyo
to buy a ticket	표를 사다 pyo-reul sa-da
ticket price	표 가격 pyo ga-gyeok
Where to?	어디까지 가세요? eo-di-kka-ji ga-se-yo?
To what station?	어느 역까지 가세요? eo-neu yeok-kka-ji ga-se-yo?
I need ...	··· 필요해요. ... pi-ryo-hae-yo.
one ticket	표 한 장 pyo han jang
two tickets	표 두 장 pyo du jang
three tickets	표 세 장 pyo se jang
one-way	편도 pyeon-do
round-trip	왕복 wang-bok
first class	일등석 il-deung-seok
second class	이등석 i-deung-seok
today	오늘 o-neul
tomorrow	내일 nae-il
the day after tomorrow	모레 mo-re
in the morning	아침에 a-chim-e
in the afternoon	오후에 o-hu-e
in the evening	저녁에 jeo-nyeo-ge

aisle seat	복도 좌석 bok-do jwa-seok
window seat	창가 좌석 chang-ga jwa-seok
How much?	얼마예요? eol-ma-ye-yo?
Can I pay by credit card?	신용카드 돼요? si-nyong-ka-deu dwae-yo?

Bus

bus	버스 beo-seu
intercity bus	시외버스 si-oe-beo-seu
bus stop	버스 정류장 beo-seu jeong-nyu-jang
Where's the nearest bus stop?	가까운 버스 정류장이 어디예요? ga-kka-un beo-seu jeong-nyu-jang-i eo-di-ye-yo?

number (bus ~, etc.)	번호 beon-ho
Which bus do I take to get to …?	…에 가려면 어느 버스를 타야 해요? … e ga-ryeo-myeon eo-neu beo-seu-reul ta-ya hae-yo?
Does this bus go to …?	이 버스 … 가요? i beo-seu … ga-yo?
How frequent are the buses?	버스는 얼마나 자주 와요? beo-seu-neun eol-ma-na ja-ju wa-yo?

every 15 minutes	십오 분 마다 si-bo bun ma-da
every half hour	삼십 분 마다 sam-sip bun ma-da
every hour	한 시간 마다 han si-gan ma-da
several times a day	하루에 여러 번 ha-ru-e yeo-reo beon
… times a day	하루에 …번 ha-ru-e …beon

schedule	시간표 si-gan-pyo
Where can I see the schedule?	시간표는 어디서 볼 수 있어요? si-gan-pyo-neun eo-di-seo bol su i-seo-yo?
When is the next bus?	다음 버스는 언제인가요? da-eum beo-seu-neun eon-je-in-ga-yo?
When is the first bus?	첫 버스는 언제인가요? cheot beo-seu-neun eon-je-in-ga-yo?

When is the last bus?

마지막 버스는
언제인가요?
ma-ji-mak beo-seu-neun
eon-je-in-ga-yo?

stop

정류장
jeong-nyu-jang

next stop

다음 정류장
da-eum jeong-nyu-jang

last stop (terminus)

종점
jong-jeom

Stop here, please.

여기에 세워 주세요.
yeo-gi-e se-wo ju-se-yo.

Excuse me, this is my stop.

실례합니다, 저 여기서
내려요.
sil-lye-ham-ni-da, jeo yeo-gi-seo
nae-ryeo-yo.

Train

train	기차 gi-cha
suburban train	교외 전차 gyo-oe jeon-cha
long-distance train	장거리 기차 jang-geo-ri gi-cha
train station	기차역 gi-cha-yeok
Excuse me, where is the exit to the platform?	실례합니다, 플랫폼으로 가는 출구가 어디인가요? sil-lye-ham-ni-da, peul-laet-po-meu-ro ga-neun chul-gu-ga eo-di-in-ga-yo?

Does this train go to ...?	이 기차 …에 가요? i gi-cha ...e ga-yo?
next train	다음 기차 da-eum gi-cha
When is the next train?	다음 기차는 언제인가요? da-eum gi-cha-neun eon-je-in-ga-yo?
Where can I see the schedule?	시간표는 어디서 볼 수 있어요? si-gan-pyo-neun eo-di-seo bol su i-seo-yo?
From which platform?	어느 플랫폼에서 출발해요? eo-neu peul-laet-pom-e-seo chul-bal-hae-yo?
When does the train arrive in ...?	기차가 …에 언제 도착해요? gi-cha-ga ...e eon-je do-chak-ae-yo?

Please help me.	도와주세요. do-wa-ju-se-yo.
I'm looking for my seat.	제 좌석을 찾고 있어요. je jwa-seo-geul chat-go i-seo-yo.
We're looking for our seats.	우리 좌석을 찾고 있어요. u-ri jwa-seo-geul chat-go i-seo-yo.

My seat is taken.	제 좌석에 다른 사람이 있어요. je jwa-seo-ge da-reun sa-ram-i i-seo-yo.
Our seats are taken.	우리 좌석에 다른 사람이 있어요. u-ri jwa-seo-ge da-reun sa-ram-i i-seo-yo.

I'm sorry but this is my seat.

죄송하지만 여긴 제
좌석이에요.
joe-song-ha-ji-man nyeo-gin je
jwa-seo-gi-ye-yo.

Is this seat taken?

이 좌석 비었나요?
i jwa-seok bi-eon-na-yo?

May I sit here?

여기 앉아도 되나요?
yeo-gi an-ja-do doe-na-yo?

On the train. Dialogue (No ticket)

Ticket, please.	표 보여주세요. pyo bo-yeo-ju-se-yo.
I don't have a ticket.	표가 없어요. pyo-ga eop-seo-yo.
I lost my ticket.	표를 잃어버렸어요. pyo-reul ri-reo-beo-ryeo-seo-yo.
I forgot my ticket at home.	표를 집에 두고 왔어요. pyo-reul ji-be du-go wa-seo-yo.

You can buy a ticket from me.	저한테 표를 사실 수 있어요. jeo-han-te pyo-reul sa-sil su i-seo-yo.
You will also have to pay a fine.	벌금도 내셔야 해요. beol-geum-do nae-syeo-ya hae-yo.
Okay.	알았어요. a-ra-seo-yo.
Where are you going?	어디까지 가세요? eo-di-kka-ji ga-se-yo?
I'm going to ...	…에 가고 있어요. ... e ga-go i-seo-yo.

How much? I don't understand.	얼마예요? 못 알아들었어요. eol-ma-ye-yo? mot a-ra-deu-reo-seo-yo.
Write it down, please.	적어 주세요. jeo-geo ju-se-yo.
Okay. Can I pay with a credit card?	알았어요. 신용카드 돼요? a-ra-seo-yo. si-nyong-ka-deu dwae-yo?
Yes, you can.	네, 돼요. ne, dwae-yo.

Here's your receipt.	영수증 여기 있어요. yeong-su-jeung yeo-gi i-seo-yo.
Sorry about the fine.	벌금을 내게 되어서 유감이예요. beol-geu-meul lae-ge doe-eo-seo yu-gam-i-ye-yo.
That's okay. It was my fault.	괜찮아요. 제 잘못이예요. gwaen-cha-na-yo. je jal-mo-si-ye-yo.
Enjoy your trip.	즐거운 여행 되세요. jeul-geo-un nyeo-haeng doe-se-yo.

Taxi

taxi	택시 taek-si
taxi driver	택시 운전사 taek-si un-jeon-sa
to catch a taxi	택시를 잡다 taek-si-reul jap-da
taxi stand	택시 정류장 taek-si jeong-nyu-jang
Where can I get a taxi?	어디서 택시를 탈 수 있어요? eo-di-seo taek-si-reul tal su i-seo-yo?
to call a taxi	택시를 부르다. taek-si-reul bu-reu-da.
I need a taxi.	택시가 필요해요. taek-si-ga pi-ryo-hae-yo.
Right now.	지금 당장. ji-geum dang-jang.
What is your address (location)?	주소가 어디예요? ju-so-ga eo-di-ye-yo?
My address is ...	제 주소는 ...예요. je ju-so-neun ...ye-yo.
Your destination?	목적지가 어디예요? mok-jeok-ji-ga eo-di-ye-yo?
Excuse me, ...	실례합니다, ... sil-lye-ham-ni-da, ...
Are you available?	타도 돼요? ta-do dwae-yo?
How much is it to get to ...?	...까지 얼마예요? ...kka-ji eol-ma-ye-yo?
Do you know where it is?	여기가 어딘지 아세요? yeo-gi-ga eo-din-ji a-se-yo?
Airport, please.	공항까지 가 주세요. gong-hang-kka-ji ga ju-se-yo.
Stop here, please.	여기에 세워 주세요. yeo-gi-e se-wo ju-se-yo.
It's not here.	여기가 아니예요. yeo-gi-ga a-ni-ye-yo.
This is the wrong address.	잘못된 주소예요. jal-mot-doen ju-so-ye-yo.
Turn left.	왼쪽으로 가세요. oen-jjo-geu-ro ga-se-yo.

Turn right.	오른쪽으로 가세요. o-reun-jjo-geu-ro ga-se-yo.
How much do I owe you?	얼마 내야 해요? eol-ma nae-ya hae-yo?
I'd like a receipt, please.	영수증 주세요. yeong-su-jeung ju-se-yo.
Keep the change.	잔돈은 가지세요. jan-do-neun ga-ji-se-yo.

Would you please wait for me?	기다려 주시겠어요? gi-da-ryeo ju-si-ge-seo-yo?
five minutes	오분 o-bun
ten minutes	십분 sip-bun
fifteen minutes	십오 분 si-bo bun
twenty minutes	이십분 i-sip-bun
half an hour	삼십분 sam-sip bun

Hotel

Hello.
안녕하세요.
an-nyeong-ha-se-yo.

My name is …
제 이름은 … 입니다.
je i-reu-meun … im-ni-da.

I have a reservation.
예약했어요.
ye-yak-ae-seo-yo.

I need …
… 필요해요.
… pi-ryo-hae-yo.

a single room
싱글 룸 하나
sing-geul lum ha-na

a double room
더블 룸 하나
deo-beul lum ha-na

How much is that?
저건 얼마예요?
jeo-geon eol-ma-ye-yo?

That's a bit expensive.
그건 조금 비싸요.
geu-geon jo-geum bi-ssa-yo.

Do you have anything else?
다른 옵션 있어요?
da-reun op-syeon i-seo-yo?

I'll take it.
그걸로 할게요.
geu-geol-lo hal-ge-yo.

I'll pay in cash.
현금으로 낼게요.
hyeon-geu-meu-ro nael-ge-yo.

I've got a problem.
문제가 있어요.
mun-je-ga i-seo-yo

My … is broken.
제 … 망가졌어요.
je … mang-ga-jyeo-seo-yo.

My … is out of order.
제 … 고장났어요.
je … go-jang-na-seo-yo.

TV
텔레비전
tel-le-bi-jeon

air conditioner
에어컨
e-eo-keon

tap
수도꼭지
su-do-kkok-ji

shower
샤워기
sya-wo-gi

sink
세면대
se-myeon-dae

safe
금고
geum-go

door lock	도어락 do-eo-rak
electrical outlet	콘센트 kon-sen-teu
hairdryer	헤어 드라이어 he-eo deu-ra-i-eo

I don't have ...	… 안 나와요. … an na-wa-yo.
water	물 mul
light	전등 jeon-deung
electricity	전기 jeon-gi

Can you give me ...?	… 주실 수 있어요? … ju-sil su i-seo-yo?
a towel	수건 su-geon
a blanket	담요 da-myo
slippers	슬리퍼 seul-li-peo
a robe	가운 ga-un
shampoo	샴푸 syam-pu
soap	비누 bi-nu

I'd like to change rooms.	방을 바꾸고 싶어요. bang-eul ba-kku-go si-peo-yo.
I can't find my key.	열쇠를 못 찾겠어요. yeol-soe-reul mot chat-ge-seo-yo.
Could you open my room, please?	제 방 문을 열어주실 수 있어요? je bang mu-neul ryeo-reo-ju-sil su i-seo-yo?

Who's there?	누구세요? nu-gu-se-yo?
Come in!	들어오세요! deu-reo-o-se-yo!
Just a minute!	잠깐만요! jam-kkan-ma-nyo!

Not right now, please.	지금 당장은 안돼요. ji-geum dang-jang-eun an-dwae-yo.
Come to my room, please.	제 방으로 와 주세요. je bang-eu-ro wa ju-se-yo.

I'd like to order food service.

룸서비스를 받고 싶어요.
rum-seo-bi-seu-reul bat-go si-peo-yo.

My room number is …

제 방 번호는 …예요.
je bang beon-ho-neun ...ye-yo.

I'm leaving …

저는 …에 떠나요.
jeo-neun ... e tteo-na-yo.

We're leaving …

우리는 …에 떠나요.
u-ri-neun ...e tteo-na-yo.

right now

지금 당장
ji-geum dang-jang

this afternoon

오늘 오후
o-neul ro-hu

tonight

오늘밤
o-neul-bam

tomorrow

내일
nae-il

tomorrow morning

내일 아침
nae-il ra-chim

tomorrow evening

내일 저녁
nae-il jeo-nyeok

the day after tomorrow

모레
mo-re

I'd like to pay.

계산하고 싶어요.
gye-san-ha-go si-peo-yo.

Everything was wonderful.

전부 다 아주 좋았어요.
jeon-bu da a-ju jo-a-seo-yo.

Where can I get a taxi?

어디서 택시를 탈 수 있어요?
eo-di-seo taek-si-reul tal su i-seo-yo?

Would you call a taxi for me, please?

택시 불러주실 수 있어요?
taek-si bul-leo-ju-sil su i-seo-yo?

Restaurant

Can I look at the menu, please?	메뉴판 볼 수 있어요? me-nyu-pan bol su i-seo-yo?
Table for one.	한 명이요. han myeong-i-yo.
There are two (three, four) of us.	두 (세, 네) 명이요. du (se, ne) myeong-i-yo.

Smoking	흡연 heu-byeon
No smoking	금연 geu-myeon
Excuse me! (addressing a waiter)	저기요! jeo-gi-yo!
menu	메뉴판 me-nyu-pan
wine list	와인 리스트 wa-in li-seu-teu
The menu, please.	메뉴판 주세요. me-nyu-pan ju-se-yo.

Are you ready to order?	주문하시겠어요? ju-mun-ha-si-ge-seo-yo?
What will you have?	어떤 걸로 하시겠어요? eo-tteon geol-lo ha-si-ge-seo-yo?
I'll have ...	저는 … 할게요. jeo-neun ... hal-ge-yo.

I'm a vegetarian.	저는 채식주의자예요. jeo-neun chae-sik-ju-ui-ja-ye-yo.
meat	고기 go-gi
fish	생선 saeng-seon
vegetables	채소 chae-so

Do you have vegetarian dishes?	채식 메뉴 있어요? chae-sik me-nyu i-seo-yo?
I don't eat pork.	돼지고기 못 먹어요. dwae-ji-go-gi mot meo-geo-yo.
He /she/ doesn't eat meat.	그는 /그녀는/ 고기 못 드세요. geu-neun /geu-nyeo-neun/ go-gi mot deu-se-yo.

I am allergic to ...

저 …에 알러지 있어요.
jeo ...e al-leo-ji i-seo-yo.

Would you please bring me ...

… 가져다 주시겠어요?
... ga-jyeo-da ju-si-ge-seo-yo?

salt | pepper | sugar

소금 | 후추 | 설탕
so-geum | hu-chu | seol-tang

coffee | tea | dessert

커피 | 차 | 디저트
keo-pi | cha | di-jeo-teu

water | sparkling | plain

물 | 탄산수 | 생수
mul | tan-san-su | saeng-su

a spoon | fork | knife

숟가락 | 포크 | 나이프
sut-ga-rak | po-keu | na-i-peu

a plate | napkin

앞접시 | 휴지
ap-jeop-si | hyu-ji

Enjoy your meal!

맛있게 드세요!
man-nit-ge deu-se-yo!

One more, please.

하나 더 주세요.
ha-na deo ju-se-yo.

It was very delicious.

아주 맛있었어요.
a-ju man-ni-seo-seo-yo.

check | change | tip

계산서 | 거스름돈 | 팁
gye-san-seo | geo-seu-reum-don | tip

Check, please.
(Could I have the check, please?)

계산서 주세요.
gye-san-seo ju-se-yo.

Can I pay by credit card?

신용카드 돼요?
si-nyong-ka-deu dwae-yo?

I'm sorry, there's a mistake here.

죄송한데 여기
잘못됐어요.
joe-song-han-de yeo-gi
jal-mot-dwae-seo-yo.

Shopping

Can I help you?
도와드릴까요?
do-wa-deu-ril-kka-yo?

Do you have …?
… 있으세요?
… i-seu-se-yo?

I'm looking for …
… 찾고 있어요.
… chat-go i-seo-yo.

I need …
… 필요해요.
… pi-ryo-hae-yo.

I'm just looking.
그냥 구경중이예요.
geu-nyang gu-gyeong-jung-i-ye-yo.

We're just looking.
우리 그냥 구경중이예요.
u-ri geu-nyang gu-gyeong-jung-i-ye-yo.

I'll come back later.
나중에 다시 올게요.
na-jung-e da-si ol-ge-yo.

We'll come back later.
우리 나중에 다시 올게요.
u-ri na-jung-e da-si ol-ge-yo.

discounts | sale
할인 | 세일
ha-rin | se-il

Would you please show me …
… 보여주세요.
… bo-yeo-ju-se-yo.

Would you please give me …
… 주세요.
… ju-se-yo.

Can I try it on?
입어봐도 돼요?
i-beo-bwa-do dwae-yo?

Excuse me, where's the fitting room?
실례합니다, 피팅 룸 어디
있어요?
sil-lye-ham-ni-da, pi-ting num eo-di
i-seo-yo?

Which color would you like?
다른 색도 있어요?
da-reun saek-do i-seo-yo?

size | length
사이즈 | 길이
sa-i-jeu | gi-ri

How does it fit?
이거 저한테 맞아요?
i-geo jeo-han-te ma-ja-yo?

How much is it?
얼마예요?
eol-ma-ye-yo?

That's too expensive.
너무 비싸요.
neo-mu bi-ssa-yo.

I'll take it.
그걸로 할게요.
geu-geol-lo hal-ge-yo.

Excuse me, where do I pay?

실례합니다, 계산 어디서
해요?
sil-lye-ham-ni-da, gye-san eo-di-seo
hae-yo?

Will you pay in cash or credit card?

현금으로 하시겠어요
카드로 하시겠어요?
hyeon-geu-meu-ro ha-si-ge-seo-yo
ka-deu-ro ha-si-ge-seo-yo?

In cash | with credit card

현금으로요 | 카드로요
hyeon-geu-meu-ro-yo | ka-deu-ro-yo

Do you want the receipt?

영수증 드릴까요?
yeong-su-jeung deu-ril-kka-yo?

Yes, please.

네, 주세요.
ne, ju-se-yo.

No, it's OK.

아니오, 괜찮아요.
a-ni-o, gwaen-cha-na-yo.

Thank you. Have a nice day!

감사합니다. 즐거운 하루
되세요!
gam-sa-ham-ni-da. jeul-geo-un ha-ru
doe-se-yo!

In town

Excuse me, please.	실례합니다, 저기요. sil-lye-ham-ni-da, jeo-gi-yo.
I'm looking for ...	··· 찾고 있어요. ... chat-go i-seo-yo.
the subway	지하철 ji-ha-cheol
my hotel	제 호텔 je ho-tel
the movie theater	영화관 yeong-hwa-gwan
a taxi stand	택시 정류장 taek-si jeong-nyu-jang

an ATM	현금인출기 hyeon-geum-in-chul-gi
a foreign exchange office	환전소 hwan-jeon-so
an internet café	피씨방 pi-ssi-bang
... street	···로 ...ro
this place	여기 yeo-gi

Do you know where ... is?	··· 어디인지 아세요? ... eo-di-in-ji a-se-yo?
Which street is this?	여기가 어디예요? yeo-gi-ga eo-di-ye-yo?
Show me where we are right now.	지금 우리가 있는 곳을 보여주세요. ji-geum u-ri-ga in-neun gos-eul bo-yeo-ju-se-yo.
Can I get there on foot?	걸어갈 수 있어요? geo-reo-gal su i-seo-yo?
Do you have a map of the city?	시내 지도 있어요? si-nae ji-do i-seo-yo?

How much is a ticket to get in?	입장권 얼마예요? ip-jang-gwon eol-ma-ye-yo?
Can I take pictures here?	사진 찍어도 돼요? sa-jin jji-geo-do dwae-yo?
Are you open?	열었어요? yeo-reo-seo-yo?

When do you open?

언제 열어요?
eon-je yeo-reo-yo?

When do you close?

언제 닫아요?
eon-je da-da-yo?

Money

money	돈 don
cash	현금 hyeon-geum
paper money	지폐 ji-pye
loose change	동전 dong-jeon
check | change | tip	계산서 | 거스름돈 | 팁 gye-san-seo | geo-seu-reum-don | tip
credit card	카드 ka-deu
wallet	지갑 ji-gap
to buy	사다 sa-da
to pay	내다 nae-da
fine	벌금 beol-geum
free	무료 mu-ryo
Where can I buy ...?	… 어디서 살 수 있어요? … eo-di-seo sal su i-seo-yo?
Is the bank open now?	은행 지금 열었어요? eun-haeng ji-geum myeo-reo-seo-yo?
When does it open?	언제 열어요? eon-je yeo-reo-yo?
When does it close?	언제 닫아요? eon-je da-da-yo?
How much?	얼마예요? eol-ma-ye-yo?
How much is this?	이건 얼마예요? i-geon eol-ma-ye-yo?
That's too expensive.	너무 비싸요. neo-mu bi-ssa-yo.
Excuse me, where do I pay?	실례합니다, 계산 어디서 해요? sil-lye-ham-ni-da, gye-san eo-di-seo hae-yo?

Check, please.

계산서 주세요.
gye-san-seo ju-se-yo.

Can I pay by credit card?

신용카드 돼요?
si-nyong-ka-deu dwae-yo?

Is there an ATM here?

여기 현금인출기 있어요?
yeo-gi hyeon-geum-in-chul-gi i-seo-yo?

I'm looking for an ATM.

현금 인출기를 찾고
있어요.
hyeon-geum in-chul-gi-reul chat-go
i-seo-yo.

I'm looking for a foreign exchange office.

환전소 찾고 있어요.
hwan-jeon-so chat-go i-seo-yo.

I'd like to change ...

··· 환전하고 싶어요.
... hwan-jeon-ha-go si-peo-yo.

What is the exchange rate?

환율 얼마예요?
hwa-nyul reol-ma-ye-yo?

Do you need my passport?

여권 필요해요?
yeo-gwon pi-ryo-hae-yo?

Time

What time is it?	지금 몇 시예요? ji-geum myeot si-ye-yo?
When?	언제요? eon-je-yo?
At what time?	몇 시예요? myeot si-e-yo?
now | later | after ...	지금 | 나중에 | … 이후에 ji-geum | na-jung-e | ... i-hu-e
one o'clock	한 시 han si
one fifteen	한 시 십오 분 han si si-bo bun
one thirty	한 시 삼십 분 han si sam-sip bun
one forty-five	한 시 사십오 분 han si sa-si-bo bun
one | two | three	한 | 두 | 세 han | du | se
four | five | six	네 | 다섯 | 여섯 ne | da-seot | yeo-seot
seven | eight | nine	일곱 | 여덟 | 아홉 il-gop | yeo-deol | a-hop
ten | eleven | twelve	열 | 열한 | 열두 yeol | yeol-han | yeol-du
in ...	… 안에 … an-e
five minutes	오분 o-bun
ten minutes	십분 sip-bun
fifteen minutes	십오분 si-bo bun
twenty minutes	이십분 i-sip-bun
half an hour	삼십분 sam-sip bun
an hour	한 시간 han si-gan
in the morning	아침에 a-chim-e
early in the morning	아침 일찍 a-chim il-jjik

this morning · 오늘 아침
o-neul ra-chim

tomorrow morning · 내일 아침
nae-il ra-chim

in the middle of the day · 한낮에
han-na-je

in the afternoon · 오후에
o-hu-e

in the evening · 저녁에
jeo-nyeo-ge

tonight · 오늘밤
o-neul-bam

at night · 밤에
bam-e

yesterday · 어제
eo-je

today · 오늘
o-neul

tomorrow · 내일
nae-il

the day after tomorrow · 모레
mo-re

What day is it today? · 오늘이 무슨 요일이예요?
o-neu-ri mu-seun nyo-i-ri-ye-yo?

It's ... · … 예요.
… ye-yo.

Monday · 월요일
wo-ryo-il

Tuesday · 화요일
hwa-yo-il

Wednesday · 수요일
su-yo-il

Thursday · 목요일
mo-gyo-il

Friday · 금요일
geu-myo-il

Saturday · 토요일
to-yo-il

Sunday · 일요일
i-ryo-il

Greetings. Introductions

Hello.	안녕하세요. an-nyeong-ha-se-yo.
Pleased to meet you.	만나서 기쁩니다. man-na-seo gi-ppeum-ni-da.
Me too.	저도요. jeo-do-yo.
I'd like you to meet ...	··· 소개합니다. ... so-gae-ham-ni-da.
Nice to meet you.	만나서 반갑습니다. man-na-seo ban-gap-seum-ni-da.
How are you?	잘 지내셨어요? jal ji-nae-syeo-seo-yo?
My name is ...	제 이름은 ··· 입니다. je i-reu-meun ... im-ni-da.
His name is ...	그의 이름은 ··· 예요. geu-ui i-reu-meun ... ye-yo.
Her name is ...	그녀의 이름은 ··· 예요. geu-nyeo-ui i-reu-meun ... ye-yo.
What's your name?	성함이 어떻게 되세요? seong-ham-i eo-tteo-ke doe-se-yo?
What's his name?	그분 성함이 뭐예요? geu-bun seong-ham-i mwo-ye-yo?
What's her name?	그분 성함이 뭐예요? geu-bun seong-ham-i mwo-ye-yo?
What's your last name?	성이 어떻게 되세요? seong-i eo-tteo-ke doe-se-yo?
You can call me ...	··· 라고 불러 주세요. ... ra-go bul-leo ju-se-yo.
Where are you from?	어디서 오셨어요? eo-di-seo o-syeo-seo-yo?
I'm from ...	··· 에서 왔어요. ... e-seo wa-seo-yo.
What do you do for a living?	무슨 일 하세요? mu-seun il ha-se-yo?
Who is this?	이 분은 누구세요? i bu-neun nu-gu-se-yo?
Who is he?	그 분은 누구세요? geu bu-neun nu-gu-se-yo?
Who is she?	그 분은 누구세요? geu bu-neun nu-gu-se-yo?

Who are they?	그 분들은 누구세요? geu bun-deu-reun nu-gu-se-yo?
This is …	이 쪽은 … 예요. i jjo-geun ... ye-yo.
my friend (masc.)	제 친구 je chin-gu
my friend (fem.)	제 친구 je chin-gu
my husband	제 남편 je nam-pyeon
my wife	제 아내 je a-nae
my father	제 아버지 je a-beo-ji
my mother	제 어머니 je eo-meo-ni
my son	제 아들 je a-deul
my daughter	제 딸 je ttal
This is our son.	이 쪽은 우리 아들이예요. i jjo-geun u-ri a-deu-ri-ye-yo.
This is our daughter.	이 쪽은 우리 딸이예요. i jjo-geun u-ri tta-ri-ye-yo.
These are my children.	이 쪽은 제 아이들이예요. i jjo-geun je a-i-deu-ri-ye-yo.
These are our children.	이 쪽은 우리 아이들이예요. i jjo-geun u-ri a-i-deu-ri-ye-yo.

Farewells

Good bye!	안녕히 계세요! an-nyeong-hi gye-se-yo!
Bye! (inform.)	안녕! an-nyeong!
See you tomorrow.	내일 만나요. nae-il man-na-yo.
See you soon.	곧 만나요. got man-na-yo.
See you at seven.	일곱 시에 만나요. il-gop si-e man-na-yo.
Have fun!	재밌게 놀아! jae-mit-ge no-ra!
Talk to you later.	나중에 봐. na-jung-e bwa.
Have a nice weekend.	주말 잘 보내. ju-mal jal bo-nae.
Good night.	안녕히 주무세요. an-nyeong-hi ju-mu-se-yo.
It's time for me to go.	갈 시간이에요. gal si-gan-i-ye-yo.
I have to go.	가야 해요. ga-ya hae-yo.
I will be right back.	금방 다시 올게요. geum-bang da-si ol-ge-yo.
It's late.	늦었어요. neu-jeo-seo-yo.
I have to get up early.	일찍 일어나야 해요. il-jjik gi-reo-na-ya hae-yo.
I'm leaving tomorrow.	내일 떠나요. nae-il tteo-na-yo.
We're leaving tomorrow.	우리는 내일 떠나요. u-ri-neun nae-il tteo-na-yo.
Have a nice trip!	즐거운 여행 되세요! jeul-geo-un nyeo-haeng doe-se-yo!
It was nice meeting you.	만나서 반가웠어요. man-na-seo ban-ga-wo-seo-yo.
It was nice talking to you.	이야기하느라 즐거웠어요. i-ya-gi-ha-neu-ra jeul-geo-wo-seo-yo.
Thanks for everything.	전부 다 감사합니다. jeon-bu da gam-sa-ham-ni-da.

I had a very good time.

아주 즐거웠어요.
a-ju jeul-geo-wo-seo-yo.

We had a very good time.

우리는 아주 즐거웠어요.
u-ri-neun a-ju jeul-geo-wo-seo-yo.

It was really great.

정말 멋졌어요.
jeong-mal meot-jyeo-seo-yo.

I'm going to miss you.

보고 싶을 거예요.
bo-go si-peul geo-ye-yo.

We're going to miss you.

우리는 당신이 보고 싶을
거예요.
u-ri-neun dang-sin-i bo-go si-peul
geo-ye-yo.

Good luck!

행운을 빌어!
haeng-u-neul bi-reo!

Say hi to ...

··· 에게 안부 전해 주세요.
... e-ge an-bu jeon-hae ju-se-yo.

Foreign language

I don't understand.	**못 알아들었어요.** mot a-ra-deu-reo-seo-yo.
Write it down, please.	**적어 주세요.** jeo-geo ju-se-yo.
Do you speak ...?	**··· 하실 수 있어요?** ... ha-sil su i-seo-yo?
I speak a little bit of ...	**저는 ··· 조금 할 수 있어요.** jeo-neun ... jo-geum hal su i-seo-yo.
English	**영어** yeong-eo
Turkish	**터키어** teo-ki-eo
Arabic	**아랍어** a-ra-beo
French	**프랑스어** peu-rang-seu-eo
German	**독일어** do-gi-reo
Italian	**이탈리아어** i-tal-li-a-eo
Spanish	**스페인어** seu-pe-in-eo
Portuguese	**포르투갈어** po-reu-tu-ga-reo
Chinese	**중국어** jung-gu-geo
Japanese	**일본어** il-bon-eo
Can you repeat that, please.	**다시 한 번 말해 주세요.** da-si han beon mal-hae ju-se-yo.
I understand.	**알아들었어요.** a-ra-deu-reo-seo-yo.
I don't understand.	**못 알아들었어요.** mot a-ra-deu-reo-seo-yo.
Please speak more slowly.	**좀 더 천천히 말해 주세요.** jom deo cheon-cheon-hi mal-hae ju-se-yo.

Is that correct? (Am I saying it right?)　　이거 맞아요?
i-geo ma-ja-yo?

What is this? (What does this mean?)　　이게 뭐예요?
i-ge mwo-ye-yo?

Apologies

Excuse me, please.	실례합니다, 저기요. sil-lye-ham-ni-da, jeo-gi-yo.
I'm sorry.	죄송합니다. joe-song-ham-ni-da.
I'm really sorry.	정말 죄송합니다. jeong-mal joe-song-ham-ni-da.
Sorry, it's my fault.	죄송해요, 제 잘못이예요. joe-song-hae-yo, je jal-mo-si-ye-yo.
My mistake.	제 실수예요. je sil-su-ye-yo.
May I ...?	…해도 되나요? ... hae-do doe-na-yo?
Do you mind if I ...?	…해도 괜찮으세요? ...hae-do gwaen-cha-neu-se-yo?
It's OK.	괜찮아요. gwaen-cha-na-yo.
It's all right.	괜찮아요. gwaen-cha-na-yo.
Don't worry about it.	걱정하지 마세요. geok-jeong-ha-ji ma-se-yo.

Agreement

Yes.	네. ne.
Yes, sure.	네, 물론입니다. ne, mul-lon-im-ni-da.
OK (Good!)	좋아요. jo-a-yo.
Very well.	아주 좋아요. a-ju jo-a-yo.
Certainly!	당연합니다! dang-yeon-ham-ni-da!
I agree.	동의해요. dong-ui-hae-yo.

That's correct.	정확해요. jeong-hwak-ae-yo.
That's right.	그게 맞아요. geu-ge ma-ja-yo.
You're right.	당신이 맞아요. dang-sin-i ma-ja-yo.
I don't mind.	저는 신경 쓰지 않아요. jeo-neun sin-gyeong sseu-ji a-na-yo.
Absolutely right.	확실히 맞아요. hwak-sil-hi ma-ja-yo.

It's possible.	가능해요. ga-neung-hae-yo.
That's a good idea.	좋은 생각이에요. jo-eun saeng-ga-gi-ye-yo.
I can't say no.	아니라고 할 수 없어요. a-ni-ra-go hal su eop-seo-yo.
I'd be happy to.	기쁘게 할게요. gi-ppeu-ge hal-ge-yo.
With pleasure.	기꺼이요. gi-kkeo-i-yo.

Refusal. Expressing doubt

No.	아니오. a-ni-o.
Certainly not.	절대 아니예요. jeol-dae a-ni-ye-yo.
I don't agree.	동의할 수 없어요. dong-ui-hal su eop-seo-yo.
I don't think so.	그렇게 생각 안 해요. geu-reo-ke saeng-gak gan hae-yo.
It's not true.	그렇지 않아요. geu-reo-chi a-na-yo.

You are wrong.	틀렸어요. teul-lyeo-seo-yo.
I think you are wrong.	틀리신 거 같아요. teul-li-sin geo ga-ta-yo.
I'm not sure.	잘 모르겠어요. jal mo-reu-ge-seo-yo.
It's impossible.	불가능해요. bul-ga-neung-hae-yo.
Nothing of the kind (sort)!	그럴 리가요! geu-reol li-ga-yo!

The exact opposite.	정 반대예요. jeong ban-dae-ye-yo.
I'm against it.	저는 반대예요. jeo-neun ban-dae-ye-yo.
I don't care.	저는 신경 안 써요. jeo-neun sin-gyeong an sseo-yo.
I have no idea.	모르겠어요. mo-reu-ge-seo-yo.
I doubt it.	그건 아닌 것 같아요. geu-geon a-nin geot ga-ta-yo.

Sorry, I can't.	죄송합니다. 못 해요. joe-song-ham-ni-da. mot tae-yo.
Sorry, I don't want to.	죄송합니다. 하기 싫어요. joe-song-ham-ni-da. ha-gi si-reo-yo.

Thank you, but I don't need this.	감사합니다, 하지만 필요 없어요. gam-sa-ham-ni-da, ha-ji-man pi-ryo eop-seo-yo.
It's getting late.	좀 늦었네요. jom neu-jeon-ne-yo.

I have to get up early.

일찍 일어나야 해요.
il-jjik gi-reo-na-ya hae-yo.

I don't feel well.

몸이 안 좋아요.
mom-i an jo-a-yo.

Expressing gratitude

Thank you.

감사합니다.
gam-sa-ham-ni-da.

Thank you very much.

대단히 감사합니다.
dae-dan-hi gam-sa-ham-ni-da.

I really appreciate it.

정말로 감사히
생각해요.
jeong-mal-lo gam-sa-hi
saeng-gak-ae-yo.

I'm really grateful to you.

당신에게 정말로
감사해요.
dang-sin-e-ge jeong-mal-lo
gam-sa-hae-yo.

We are really grateful to you.

저희는 당신에게 정말로
감사해요.
jeo-hui-neun dang-sin-e-ge jeong-mal-lo
gam-sa-hae-yo.

Thank you for your time.

시간 내 주셔서
감사합니다.
si-gan nae ju-syeo-seo
gam-sa-ham-ni-da.

Thanks for everything.

전부 다 감사합니다.
jeon-bu da gam-sa-ham-ni-da.

Thank you for ...

···에 대해 감사합니다.
...e dae-hae gam-sa-ham-ni-da.

your help

도움
do-um

a nice time

즐거운 시간
jeul-geo-un si-gan

a wonderful meal

훌륭한 식사
hul-lyung-han sik-sa

a pleasant evening

만족스러운 저녁
man-jok-seu-reo-un jeo-nyeok

a wonderful day

훌륭한 하루
hul-lyung-han ha-ru

an amazing journey

근사한 여행
geun-sa-han nyeo-haeng

Don't mention it.

별 말씀을요.
byeol mal-sseu-meu-ryo.

You are welcome.

천만에요.
cheon-man-e-yo.

Any time.

언제든지요.
eon-je-deun-ji-yo.

My pleasure.

제가 즐거웠어요.
je-ga jeul-geo-wo-seo-yo.

Forget it.

됐어요.
dwae-seo-yo.

Don't worry about it.

걱정하지 마세요.
geok-jeong-ha-ji ma-se-yo.

Congratulations. Best wishes

Congratulations!

축하합니다!
chuk-a-ham-ni-da!

Happy birthday!

생일 축하합니다!
saeng-il chuk-a-ham-ni-da!

Merry Christmas!

메리 크리스마스!
me-ri keu-ri-seu-ma-seu!

Happy New Year!

새해 복 많이 받으세요!
sae-hae bok ma-ni ba-deu-se-yo!

Happy Easter!

즐거운 부활절 되세요!
jeul-geo-un bu-hwal-jeol doe-se-yo!

Happy Hanukkah!

즐거운 하누카 되세요!
jeul-geo-un ha-nu-ka doe-se-yo!

I'd like to propose a toast.

건배해요.
geon-bae-hae-yo.

Cheers!

건배!
geon-bae!

Let's drink to ...!

··· 위하여!
... wi-ha-yeo!

To our success!

성공을 위하여!
seong-gong-eul rwi-ha-yeo!

To your success!

성공을 위하여!
seong-gong-eul rwi-ha-yeo!

Good luck!

행운을 빌어!
haeng-u-neul bi-reo!

Have a nice day!

좋은 하루 되세요!
jo-eun ha-ru doe-se-yo!

Have a good holiday!

좋은 휴일 되세요!
jo-eun hyu-il doe-se-yo!

Have a safe journey!

안전한 여행 되세요!
an-jeon-han nyeo-haeng doe-se-yo!

I hope you get better soon!

빨리 나으세요!
ppal-li na-eu-se-yo!

Socializing

Why are you sad?
왜 슬퍼하세요?
wae seul-peo-ha-se-yo?

Smile! Cheer up!
웃으세요! 기운 내세요!
us-eu-se-yo! gi-un nae-se-yo!

Are you free tonight?
오늘 밤에 시간 있으세요?
o-neul bam-e si-gan i-seu-se-yo?

May I offer you a drink?
제가 한 잔 살까요?
je-ga han jan sal-kka-yo?

Would you like to dance?
춤 추실래요?
chum chu-sil-lae-yo?

Let's go to the movies.
영화 보러 갑시다.
yeong-hwa bo-reo gap-si-da.

May I invite you to ...?
…에 초대해도 될까요?
...e cho-dae-hae-do doel-kka-yo?

a restaurant
음식점
eum-sik-jeom

the movies
영화관
yeong-hwa-gwan

the theater
극장
geuk-jang

go for a walk
산책
san-chaek

At what time?
몇 시예요?
myeot si-e-yo?

tonight
오늘밤
o-neul-bam

at six
여섯 시
yeo-seot si

at seven
일곱 시
il-gop si

at eight
여덟 시
yeo-deol si

at nine
아홉 시
a-hop si

Do you like it here?
여기가 마음에 드세요?
yeo-gi-ga ma-eum-e deu-se-yo?

Are you here with someone?
누구랑 같이 왔어요?
nu-gu-rang ga-chi wa-seo-yo?

I'm with my friend.
친구랑 같이 왔어요.
chin-gu-rang ga-chi wa-seo-yo.

I'm with my friends.	친구들이랑 같이 왔어요. chin-gu-deu-ri-rang ga-chi wa-seo-yo.
No, I'm alone.	아니오, 혼자 왔어요. a-ni-o, hon-ja wa-seo-yo.

Do you have a boyfriend?	남자친구 있어? nam-ja-chin-gu i-seo?
I have a boyfriend.	남자친구 있어. nam-ja-chin-gu i-seo.
Do you have a girlfriend?	여자친구 있어? yeo-ja-chin-gu i-seo?
I have a girlfriend.	여자친구 있어. yeo-ja-chin-gu i-seo.

Can I see you again?	다시 만날래? da-si man-nal-lae?
Can I call you?	전화해도 돼? jeon-hwa-hae-do dwae?
Call me. (Give me a call.)	전화해 줘. jeon-hwa-hae jwo.
What's your number?	전화번호가 뭐야? jeon-hwa-beon-ho-ga mwo-ya?
I miss you.	보고싶어. bo-go-si-peo.

You have a beautiful name.	이름이 아름다우시네요. i-reum-i a-reum-da-u-si-ne-yo.
I love you.	사랑해. sa-rang-hae.
Will you marry me?	결혼해 줄래? gyeol-hon-hae jul-lae?
You're kidding!	장난치지 마세요! jang-nan-chi-ji ma-se-yo!
I'm just kidding.	장난이었어요. jang-nan-i-eo-seo-yo.

Are you serious?	진심이세요? jin-sim-i-se-yo?
I'm serious.	진심이예요. jin-sim-i-ye-yo.
Really?!	정말로요?! jeong-mal-lo-yo?!
It's unbelievable!	믿을 수 없어요! mi-deul su eop-seo-yo!
I don't believe you.	당신을 믿지 않아요. dang-si-neul mit-ji a-na-yo.

I can't.	그럴 수 없어요. geu-reol su eop-seo-yo.
I don't know.	모르겠어요. mo-reu-ge-seo-yo.

I don't understand you.	무슨 말인지 모르겠어요. mu-seun ma-rin-ji mo-reu-ge-seo-yo.
Please go away.	저리 가세요. jeo-ri ga-se-yo.
Leave me alone!	혼자 있고 싶어요! hon-ja it-go si-peo-yo!

I can't stand him.	그를 견딜 수 없어요. geu-reul gyeon-dil su eop-seo-yo.
You are disgusting!	당신 역겨워요! dang-sin nyeok-gyeo-wo-yo!
I'll call the police!	경찰을 부를 거예요! gyeong-cha-reul bu-reul geo-ye-yo!

Sharing impressions. Emotions

I like it.
마음에 들어요.
ma-eum-e deu-reo-yo.

Very nice.
아주 좋아요.
a-ju jo-a-yo.

That's great!
멋져요!
meot-jyeo-yo!

It's not bad.
나쁘지 않아요.
na-ppeu-ji a-na-yo.

I don't like it.
마음에 들지 않아요.
ma-eum-e deul-ji a-na-yo.

It's not good.
좋지 않아요.
jo-chi a-na-yo.

It's bad.
나빠요.
na-ppa-yo.

It's very bad.
아주 나빠요.
a-ju na-ppa-yo.

It's disgusting.
역겨워요.
yeok-gyeo-wo-yo.

I'm happy.
저는 행복해요.
jeo-neun haeng-bok-ae-yo.

I'm content.
저는 만족해요.
jeo-neun man-jok-ae-yo.

I'm in love.
저는 사랑에 빠졌어요.
jeo-neun sa-rang-e ppa-jyeo-seo-yo.

I'm calm.
저는 침착해요.
jeo-neun chim-chak-ae-yo.

I'm bored.
저는 지루해요.
jeo-neun ji-ru-hae-yo.

I'm tired.
저는 지쳤어요.
jeo-neun ji-chyeo-seo-yo.

I'm sad.
저는 슬퍼요.
jeo-neun seul-peo-yo.

I'm frightened.
저는 무서워요.
jeo-neun mu-seo-wo-yo.

I'm angry.
저는 화났어요.
jeo-neun hwa-na-seo-yo.

I'm worried.
저는 걱정이 돼요.
jeo-neun geok-jeong-i dwae-yo.

I'm nervous.
저는 긴장이 돼요.
jeo-neun gin-jang-i dwae-yo.

I'm jealous. (envious)

저는 부러워요.
jeo-neun bu-reo-wo-yo.

I'm surprised.

놀랐어요.
nol-la-seo-yo.

I'm perplexed.

당황했어요.
dang-hwang-hae-seo-yo.

Problems. Accidents

I've got a problem.	문제가 있어요. mun-je-ga i-seo-yo.
We've got a problem.	우리는 문제가 있어요. u-ri-neun mun-je-ga i-seo-yo.
I'm lost.	길을 잃었어요. gi-reul ri-reo-seo-yo.
I missed the last bus (train).	마지막 버스 (기차)를 놓쳤어요. ma-ji-mak beo-seu (gi-cha)reul lo-chyeo-seo-yo.
I don't have any money left.	돈이 다 떨어졌어요. don-i da tteo-reo-jyeo-seo-yo.
I've lost my ...	… 잃어버렸어요. ... i-reo-beo-ryeo-seo-yo.
Someone stole my ...	제 … 누가 훔쳐갔어요. je ... nu-ga hum-chyeo-ga-seo-yo.
passport	여권 yeo-gwon
wallet	지갑 ji-gap
papers	서류 seo-ryu
ticket	표 pyo
money	돈 don
handbag	핸드백 haen-deu-baek
camera	카메라 ka-me-ra
laptop	노트북 no-teu-buk
tablet computer	타블렛피씨 ta-beul-let-pi-ssi
mobile phone	핸드폰 haen-deu-pon
Help me!	도와주세요! do-wa-ju-se-yo!
What's happened?	무슨 일이 있었어요? mu-seun i-ri i-seo-seo-yo?
fire	화재 hwa-jae

shooting	총격 chong-gyeok
murder	살인 sa-rin
explosion	폭발 pok-bal
fight	폭행 pok-aeng

Call the police!	경찰을 불러 주세요! gyeong-cha-reul bul-leo ju-se-yo!
Please hurry up!	제발 서둘러요! je-bal seo-dul-leo-yo!
I'm looking for the police station.	경찰서를 찾고 있어요. gyeong-chal-seo-reul chat-go i-seo-yo.
I need to make a call.	전화를 걸어야 해요. jeon-hwa-reul geo-reo-ya hae-yo.
May I use your phone?	전화를 빌려주실 수 있어요? jeon-hwa-reul bil-lyeo-ju-sil su i-seo-yo?

I've been ...	저는 ··· 당했어요. jeo-neun ... dang-hae-seo-yo.
mugged	강도 gang-do
robbed	도둑질 do-duk-jil
raped	강간 gang-gan
attacked (beaten up)	폭행 pok-aeng

Are you all right?	괜찮으세요? gwaen-cha-neu-se-yo?
Did you see who it was?	누구였는지 보셨어요? nu-gu-yeon-neun-ji bo-syeo-seo-yo?
Would you be able to recognize the person?	그 사람을 알아볼 수 있겠어요? geu sa-ra-meul ra-ra-bol su it-ge-seo-yo?
Are you sure?	확실해요? hwak-sil-hae-yo?

Please calm down.	제발 진정해요. je-bal jin-jeong-hae-yo.
Take it easy!	마음을 가라앉히세요! ma-eu-meul ga-ra-an-chi-se-yo!
Don't worry!	걱정하지 마세요! geok-jeong-ha-ji ma-se-yo!
Everything will be fine.	다 잘 될 거예요. da jal doel geo-ye-yo.
Everything's all right.	다 괜찮아요. da gwaen-cha-na-yo.

Come here, please.

이 쪽으로 오세요.
i jjo-geu-ro o-se-yo.

I have some questions for you.

질문이 있습니다.
jil-mun-i it-seum-ni-da.

Wait a moment, please.

잠시 기다려 주세요.
jam-si gi-da-ryeo ju-se-yo.

Do you have any I.D.?

신분증 있습니까?
sin-bun-jeung it-seum-ni-kka?

Thanks. You can leave now.

감사합니다. 이제 가셔도
됩니다.
gam-sa-ham-ni-da. i-je ga-syeo-do
doem-ni-da.

Hands behind your head!

손 머리 위로 들어!
son meo-ri wi-ro deu-reo!

You're under arrest!

체포한다!
che-po-han-da!

Health problems

Please help me.
도와주세요.
do-wa-ju-se-yo.

I don't feel well.
몸이 안 좋아요.
mom-i an jo-a-yo.

My husband doesn't feel well.
제 남편이 몸이 안 좋아요.
je nam-pyeon-i mom-i an jo-a-yo.

My son ...
제 아들이 …
je a-deu-ri ...

My father ...
제 아버지가 …
je a-beo-ji-ga ...

My wife doesn't feel well.
제 아내가 몸이 안 좋아요.
je a-nae-ga mom-i an jo-a-yo.

My daughter ...
제 딸이 …
je tta-ri ...

My mother ...
제 어머니가 …
je eo-meo-ni-ga ...

I've got a ...
…이 있어요.
...i i-seo-yo.

headache
두통
du-tong

sore throat
인후통
in-hu-tong

stomach ache
복통
bok-tong

toothache
치통
chi-tong

I feel dizzy.
어지러워요.
eo-ji-reo-wo-yo.

He has a fever.
그는 열이 있어요.
geu-neun nyeo-ri i-seo-yo.

She has a fever.
그녀는 열이 있어요.
geu-nyeo-neun nyeo-ri i-seo-yo.

I can't breathe.
숨을 못 쉬겠어요.
su-meul mot swi-ge-seo-yo.

I'm short of breath.
숨이 차요.
sum-i cha-yo.

I am asthmatic.
저는 천식이 있어요.
jeo-neun cheon-si-gi i-seo-yo.

I am diabetic.
저는 당뇨가 있어요.
jeo-neun dang-nyo-ga i-seo-yo.

I can't sleep.	저는 잠을 못 자요. jeo-neun ja-meul mot ja-yo.
food poisoning	식중독 sik-jung-dok

It hurts here.	여기가 아파요. yeo-gi-ga a-pa-yo.
Help me!	도와주세요! do-wa-ju-se-yo!
I am here!	여기 있어요! yeo-gi i-seo-yo!
We are here!	우리 여기 있어요! u-ri yeo-gi i-seo-yo!
Get me out of here!	꺼내주세요! kkeo-nae-ju-se-yo!
I need a doctor.	의사가 필요해요. ui-sa-ga pi-ryo-hae-yo.
I can't move.	못 움직이겠어요. mot um-ji-gi-ge-seo-yo.
I can't move my legs.	다리를 못 움직이겠어요. da-ri-reul mot um-ji-gi-ge-seo-yo.

I have a wound.	다쳤어요. da-chyeo-seo-yo.
Is it serious?	심각한가요? sim-gak-an-ga-yo?
My documents are in my pocket.	주머니에 제 서류가 있어요. ju-meo-ni-e je seo-ryu-ga i-seo-yo.
Calm down!	진정해요! jin-jeong-hae-yo!
May I use your phone?	전화를 빌려주실 수 있어요? jeon-hwa-reul bil-lyeo-ju-sil su i-seo-yo?

Call an ambulance!	구급차를 불러 주세요! gu-geup-cha-reul bul-leo ju-se-yo!
It's urgent!	급해요! geu-pae-yo!
It's an emergency!	긴급 상황이에요! gin-geup sang-hwang-i-e-yo!
Please hurry up!	제발 서둘러요! je-bal seo-dul-leo-yo!
Would you please call a doctor?	의사를 불러주시겠어요? ui-sa-reul bul-leo-ju-si-ge-seo-yo?
Where is the hospital?	병원은 어디 있어요? byeong-wo-neun eo-di i-seo-yo?

How are you feeling?	기분이 어떠세요? gi-bun-i eo-tteo-se-yo?
Are you all right?	괜찮으세요? gwaen-cha-neu-se-yo?
What's happened?	무슨 일이 있었어요? mu-seun i-ri i-seo-seo-yo?

I feel better now.　　　　　이제 나아졌어요.
　　　　　　　　　　　　i-je na-a-jyeo-seo-yo.

It's OK.　　　　　　　　괜찮아요.
　　　　　　　　　　　　gwaen-cha-na-yo.

It's all right.　　　　　괜찮아요.
　　　　　　　　　　　　gwaen-cha-na-yo.

At the pharmacy

pharmacy (drugstore)	약국 yak-guk
24-hour pharmacy	24시간 약국 i-sip-sa-si-gan nyak-guk
Where is the closest pharmacy?	가장 가까운 약국이 어디예요? ga-jang ga-kka-un nyak-gu-gi eo-di-ye-yo?
Is it open now?	지금 열었어요? ji-geum myeo-reo-seo-yo?
At what time does it open?	몇 시에 열어요? myeot si-e yeo-reo-yo?
At what time does it close?	몇 시에 닫아요? myeot si-e da-da-yo?
Is it far?	멀어요? meo-reo-yo?
Can I get there on foot?	걸어갈 수 있어요? geo-reo-gal su i-seo-yo?
Can you show me on the map?	지도에서 보여주실 수 있어요? ji-do-e-seo bo-yeo-ju-sil su i-seo-yo?
Please give me something for ...	···에 듣는 약 주세요. ...e deun-neun nyak ju-se-yo.
a headache	두통 du-tong
a cough	기침 gi-chim
a cold	감기 gam-gi
the flu	독감 dok-gam
a fever	열 yeol
a stomach ache	복통 bok-tong
nausea	구토 gu-to
diarrhea	설사 seol-sa
constipation	변비 byeon-bi

pain in the back	등 통증 deung tong-jeung
chest pain	가슴 통증 ga-seum tong-jeung
side stitch	옆구리 당김 yeop-gu-ri dang-gim
abdominal pain	배 통증 bae tong-jeung
pill	알약 a-ryak
ointment, cream	연고 yeon-go
syrup	물약 mul-lyak
spray	스프레이 seu-peu-re-i
drops	안약 a-nyak
You need to go to the hospital.	병원에 가셔야 해요. byeong-won-e ga-syeo-ya hae-yo.
health insurance	건강보험 geon-gang-bo-heom
prescription	처방전 cheo-bang-jeon
insect repellant	방충제 bang-chung-je
Band Aid	밴드에이드 baen-deu-e-i-deu

The bare minimum

Excuse me, ...	실례합니다, ... sil-lye-ham-ni-da, ...
Hello.	안녕하세요. an-nyeong-ha-se-yo.
Thank you.	감사합니다. gam-sa-ham-ni-da.
Good bye.	안녕히 계세요. an-nyeong-hi gye-se-yo.
Yes.	네. ne.
No.	아니오. a-ni-o.
I don't know.	모르겠어요. mo-reu-ge-seo-yo.
Where? | Where to? | When?	어디예요? | 어디까지 가세요? | 언제요? eo-di-ye-yo? | eo-di-kka-ji ga-se-yo? | eon-je-yo?

I need ...	... 필요해요. ... pi-ryo-hae-yo.
I want ...	... 싶어요. ... si-peo-yo.
Do you have ...?	... 있으세요? ... i-seu-se-yo?
Is there a ... here?	여기 ... 있어요? yeo-gi ... i-seo-yo?
May I ...?	...해도 되나요? ... hae-do doe-na-yo?
..., please (polite request)	..., 부탁합니다. ..., bu-tak-am-ni-da.

I'm looking for ...	... 찾고 있어요. ... chat-go i-seo-yo.
restroom	화장실 hwa-jang-sil
ATM	현금인출기 hyeon-geum-in-chul-gi
pharmacy (drugstore)	약국 yak-guk
hospital	병원 byeong-won
police station	경찰서 gyeong-chal-seo

subway	지하철 ji-ha-cheol
taxi	택시 taek-si
train station	기차역 gi-cha-yeok

My name is ...	제 이름은 … 입니다. je i-reu-meun ... im-ni-da.
What's your name?	성함이 어떻게 되세요? seong-ham-i eo-tteo-ke doe-se-yo?
Could you please help me?	도와주세요. do-wa-ju-se-yo.
I've got a problem.	문제가 있어요. mun-je-ga i-seo-yo.
I don't feel well.	몸이 안 좋아요. mom-i an jo-a-yo.
Call an ambulance!	구급차를 불러 주세요! gu-geup-cha-reul bul-leo ju-se-yo!
May I make a call?	전화를 써도 되나요? jeon-hwa-reul sseo-do doe-na-yo?

I'm sorry.	죄송합니다. joe-song-ham-ni-da.
You're welcome.	천만에요. cheon-man-e-yo.

I, me	저 jeo
you (inform.)	너 neo
he	그 geu
she	그녀 geu-nyeo
they (masc.)	그들 geu-deul
they (fem.)	그들 geu-deul
we	우리 u-ri
you (pl)	너희 neo-hui
you (sg, form.)	당신 dang-sin

ENTRANCE	입구 ip-gu
EXIT	출구 chul-gu
OUT OF ORDER	고장 go-jang

CLOSED

닫힘
da-chim

OPEN

열림
yeol-lim

FOR WOMEN

여성용
yeo-seong-yong

FOR MEN

남성용
nam-seong-yong

MINI DICTIONARY

This section contains 250
useful words required for
everyday communication.
You will find the names of
months and days of the week
here. The dictionary also
contains topics such as colors,
measurements, family, and
more

T&P Books Publishing

DICTIONARY CONTENTS

T&P Books Publishing

time	시간	si-gan
hour	시	si
half an hour	반시간	ban-si-gan
minute	분	bun
second	초	cho
today (adv)	오늘	o-neul
tomorrow (adv)	내일	nae-il
yesterday (adv)	어제	eo-je
Monday	월요일	wo-ryo-il
Tuesday	화요일	hwa-yo-il
Wednesday	수요일	su-yo-il
Thursday	목요일	mo-gyo-il
Friday	금요일	geu-myo-il
Saturday	토요일	to-yo-il
Sunday	일요일	i-ryo-il
day	낮	nat
working day	근무일	geun-mu-il
public holiday	공휴일	gong-hyu-il
weekend	주말	ju-mal
week	주	ju
last week (adv)	지난 주에	ji-nan ju-e
next week (adv)	다음 주에	da-eum ju-e
in the morning	아침에	a-chim-e
in the afternoon	오후에	o-hu-e
in the evening	저녁에	jeo-nyeo-ge
tonight (this evening)	오늘 저녁에	o-neul jeo-nyeo-ge
at night	밤에	bam-e
midnight	자정	ja-jeong
January	일월	i-rwol
February	이월	i-wol
March	삼월	sam-wol
April	사월	sa-wol
May	오월	o-wol
June	유월	yu-wol
July	칠월	chi-rwol
August	팔월	pa-rwol

September	구월	gu-wol
October	시월	si-wol
November	십일월	si-bi-rwol
December	십이월	si-bi-wol

in spring	봄에	bom-e
in summer	여름에	yeo-reum-e
in fall	가을에	ga-eu-re
in winter	겨울에	gyeo-u-re

month	월, 달	wol, dal
season (summer, etc.)	계절	gye-jeol
year	년	nyeon

2. Numbers. Numerals

0 zero	영	yeong
1 one	일	il
2 two	이	i
3 three	삼	sam
4 four	사	sa

5 five	오	o
6 six	육	yuk
7 seven	칠	chil
8 eight	팔	pal
9 nine	구	gu
10 ten	십	sip

11 eleven	십일	si-bil
12 twelve	십이	si-bi
13 thirteen	십삼	sip-sam
14 fourteen	십사	sip-sa
15 fifteen	십오	si-bo

16 sixteen	십육	si-byuk
17 seventeen	십칠	sip-chil
18 eighteen	십팔	sip-pal
19 nineteen	십구	sip-gu

20 twenty	이십	i-sip
30 thirty	삼십	sam-sip
40 forty	사십	sa-sip
50 fifty	오십	o-sip

60 sixty	육십	yuk-sip
70 seventy	칠십	chil-sip
80 eighty	팔십	pal-sip
90 ninety	구십	gu-sip
100 one hundred	백	baek

200 two hundred	이백	i-baek
300 three hundred	삼백	sam-baek
400 four hundred	사백	sa-baek
500 five hundred	오백	o-baek
600 six hundred	육백	yuk-baek
700 seven hundred	칠백	chil-baek
800 eight hundred	팔백	pal-baek
900 nine hundred	구백	gu-baek
1000 one thousand	천	cheon
10000 ten thousand	만	man
one hundred thousand	십만	sim-man
million	백만	baeng-man
billion	십억	si-beok

3. Humans. Family

man (adult male)	남자	nam-ja
young man	젊은 분	jeol-meun bun
woman	여자	yeo-ja
girl (young woman)	소녀, 아가씨	so-nyeo, a-ga-ssi
old man	노인	no-in
old woman	노인	no-in
mother	어머니	eo-meo-ni
father	아버지	a-beo-ji
son	아들	a-deul
daughter	딸	ttal
brother	형제	hyeong-je
sister	자매	ja-mae
parents	부모	bu-mo
child	아이, 아동	a-i, a-dong
children	아이들	a-i-deul
stepmother	계모	gye-mo
stepfather	계부	gye-bu
grandmother	할머니	hal-meo-ni
grandfather	할아버지	ha-ra-beo-ji
grandson	손자	son-ja
granddaughter	손녀	son-nyeo
grandchildren	손자들	son-ja-deul
uncle	삼촌	sam-chon
nephew	조카	jo-ka
niece	조카딸	jo-ka-ttal
wife	아내	a-nae
husband	남편	nam-pyeon

married (masc.)	결혼한	gyeol-hon-han
married (fem.)	결혼한	gyeol-hon-han
widow	과부	gwa-bu
widower	홀아비	ho-ra-bi
name (first name)	이름	i-reum
surname (last name)	성	seong
relative	친척	chin-cheok
friend (masc.)	친구	chin-gu
friendship	우정	u-jeong
partner	파트너	pa-teu-neo
superior (n)	윗사람	wit-sa-ram
colleague	동료	dong-nyo
neighbors	이웃들	i-ut-deul

4. Human body

body	몸	mom
heart	심장	sim-jang
blood	피	pi
brain	두뇌	du-noe
bone	뼈	ppyeo
spine (backbone)	등뼈	deung-ppyeo
rib	늑골	neuk-gol
lungs	폐	pye
skin	피부	pi-bu
head	머리	meo-ri
face	얼굴	eol-gul
nose	코	ko
forehead	이마	i-ma
cheek	뺨, 볼	ppyam, bol
mouth	입	ip
tongue	혀	hyeo
tooth	이	i
lips	입술	ip-sul
chin	턱	teok
ear	귀	gwi
neck	목	mok
eye	눈	nun
pupil	눈동자	nun-dong-ja
eyebrow	눈썹	nun-sseop
eyelash	속눈썹	song-nun-sseop
hair	머리털, 헤어	meo-ri-teol, he-eo
hairstyle	머리 스타일	meo-ri seu-ta-il

mustache	콧수염	kot-su-yeom
beard	턱수염	teok-su-yeom
to have (a beard, etc.)	기르다	gi-reu-da
bald (adj)	대머리인	dae-meo-ri-in

hand	손	son
arm	팔	pal
finger	손가락	son-ga-rak
nail	손톱	son-top
palm	손바닥	son-ba-dak

shoulder	어깨	eo-kkae
leg	다리	da-ri
knee	무릎	mu-reup
heel	발뒤꿈치	bal-dwi-kkum-chi
back	등	deung

5. Clothing. Personal accessories

clothes	옷	ot
coat (overcoat)	코트	ko-teu
fur coat	모피 외투	mo-pi oe-tu
jacket (e.g., leather ~)	재킷	jae-kit
raincoat (trenchcoat, etc.)	트렌치코트	teu-ren-chi-ko-teu

shirt (button shirt)	셔츠	syeo-cheu
pants	바지	ba-ji
suit jacket	재킷	jae-kit
suit	양복	yang-bok

dress (frock)	드레스	deu-re-seu
skirt	치마	chi-ma
T-shirt	티셔츠	ti-syeo-cheu
bathrobe	목욕가운	mo-gyok-ga-un
pajamas	파자마	pa-ja-ma
workwear	작업복	ja-geop-bok

underwear	속옷	so-got
socks	양말	yang-mal
bra	브라	beu-ra
pantyhose	팬티 스타킹	paen-ti seu-ta-king
stockings (thigh highs)	밴드 스타킹	baen-deu seu-ta-king
bathing suit	수영복	su-yeong-bok

hat	모자	mo-ja
footwear	신발	sin-bal
boots (e.g., cowboy ~)	부츠	bu-cheu
heel	굽	gup
shoestring	끈	kkeun
shoe polish	구두약	gu-du-yak

gloves	장갑	jang-gap
mittens	벙어리장갑	beong-eo-ri-jang-gap
scarf (muffler)	목도리	mok-do-ri
glasses (eyeglasses)	안경	an-gyeong
umbrella	우산	u-san
tie (necktie)	넥타이	nek-ta-i
handkerchief	손수건	son-su-geon
comb	빗	bit
hairbrush	빗, 솔빗	bit, sol-bit
buckle	버클	beo-keul
belt	벨트	bel-teu
purse	핸드백	haen-deu-baek

6. House. Apartment

apartment	아파트	a-pa-teu
room	방	bang
bedroom	침실	chim-sil
dining room	식당	sik-dang
living room	거실	geo-sil
study (home office)	서재	seo-jae
entry room	곁방	gyeot-bang
bathroom (room with a bath or shower)	욕실	yok-sil
half bath	화장실	hwa-jang-sil
vacuum cleaner	진공 청소기	jin-gong cheong-so-gi
mop	대걸레	dae-geol-le
dust cloth	행주	haeng-ju
short broom	빗자루	bit-ja-ru
dustpan	쓰레받기	sseu-re-bat-gi
furniture	가구	ga-gu
table	식탁, 테이블	sik-tak, te-i-beul
chair	의자	ui-ja
armchair	안락 의자	al-lak gui-ja
mirror	거울	geo-ul
carpet	양탄자	yang-tan-ja
fireplace	벽난로	byeong-nan-no
drapes	커튼	keo-teun
table lamp	테이블 램프	deung
chandelier	샹들리에	syang-deul-li-e
kitchen	부엌	bu-eok
gas stove (range)	가스 레인지	ga-seu re-in-ji
electric stove	전기 레인지	jeon-gi re-in-ji

microwave oven	전자 레인지	jeon-ja re-in-ji
refrigerator	냉장고	naeng-jang-go
freezer	냉동고	naeng-dong-go
dishwasher	식기 세척기	sik-gi se-cheok-gi
faucet	수도꼭지	su-do-kkok-ji
meat grinder	고기 분쇄기	go-gi bun-swae-gi
juicer	과즙기	gwa-jeup-gi
toaster	토스터	to-seu-teo
mixer	믹서기	mik-seo-gi
coffee machine	커피 메이커	keo-pi me-i-keo
kettle	주전자	ju-jeon-ja
teapot	티팟	ti-pat
TV set	텔레비전	tel-le-bi-jeon
VCR (video recorder)	비디오테이프 녹화기	bi-di-o-te-i-peu nok-wa-gi
iron (e.g., steam ~)	다리미	da-ri-mi
telephone	전화	jeon-hwa

www.ingramcontent.com/pod-product-compliance
Lightning Source LLC
Chambersburg PA
CBHW071505070426
42452CB00041B/2303